BRILLIANT READER

A BOOK LOG FOR KIDS [AND PARENTS]

How to use:

Grab a book, curl up, and read it!
Log your book—the basic info
(title, author, etc.) and your own
thoughts. Rate the book by filling
in the stars.
One star = b-o-r-i-n-g . . .
Ten stars = Most awesomest ever!

BOOK TITLE:

Author

Illustrator

Fiction ☐ Nonfiction ☐ # of Pages

My favorite characters in the book are . . .

_____
_____
_____
_____

My favorite part of the book is . . .

_____
_____
_____
_____
_____
_____
_____

I rate this book . . .

☆ ☆ ☆ ☆ ☆ ☆ ☆ ☆ ☆

This drawing is a scene from the book. It shows . . .

_____

_____

_____

_____

_____

_____

BOOK 👉 TITLE:

Author

Illustrator

Fiction ☐ **Nonfiction** ☐ **# of Pages**

My favorite characters in the book are . . .

_____
_____
_____
_____

My favorite part of the book is . . .

_____
_____
_____
_____
_____
_____
_____
_____

I rate this book . . .

☆ ☆ ☆ ☆ ☆ ☆ ☆ ☆ ☆ ☆

Date finished

This drawing is a scene from the book. It shows . . .

ʔAdJid5ɷK

BOOK TITLE:

Author

Illustrator

Fiction ☐ **Nonfiction** ☐ **# of Pages**

My favorite characters in the book are . . .

_____
_____
_____
_____

My favorite part of the book is . . .

_____
_____
_____
_____
_____
_____
_____
_____

I rate this book . . .

Date finished

This drawing is a scene from the book. It shows . . .
_____
_____
_____
_____
_____
_____

BOOK TITLE:

Author

Illustrator

Fiction ☐ **Nonfiction** ☐ **# of Pages**

My favorite characters in the book are . . .

_____
_____
_____
_____

My favorite part of the book is . . .

_____
_____
_____
_____
_____
_____
_____
_____

I rate this book . . .

☆ ☆ ☆ ☆ ☆ ☆ ☆ ☆ ☆

Date finished

This drawing is a scene from the book. It shows . . .

BOOK TITLE:

Author

Illustrator

Fiction ☐ Nonfiction ☐ # of Pages

My favorite characters in the book are . . .

_____
_____
_____
_____

My favorite part of the book is . . .

_____
_____
_____
_____
_____
_____
_____

I rate this book . . .

☆ ☆ ☆ ☆ ☆ ☆ ☆ ☆ ☆ ☆

Date finished

This drawing is a scene from the book. It shows . . .

BOOK TITLE:

Author

Illustrator

Fiction ☐ Nonfiction ☐   # of Pages

My favorite characters in the book are . . .

_____
_____
_____
_____

My favorite part of the book is . . .

_____
_____
_____
_____
_____
_____
_____
_____

I rate this book . . . ☆☆☆☆☆☆☆☆☆☆

Date finished

This drawing is a scene from the book. It shows . . .

BOOK TITLE:

Author

Illustrator

Fiction ☐ Nonfiction ☐ # of Pages

My favorite characters in the book are . . .

_____
_____
_____
_____

My favorite part of the book is . . .

_____
_____
_____
_____
_____
_____
_____
_____

I rate this book . . .

☆ ☆ ☆ ☆ ☆ ☆ ☆ ☆ ☆ ☆

Date finished

This drawing is a scene from the book. It shows . . .

_____

_____

_____

_____

_____

_____

BOOK TITLE:

Author

Illustrator

Fiction ☐ Nonfiction ☐ # of Pages

My favorite characters in the book are . . .

_____
_____
_____
_____
_____

My favorite part of the book is . . .

_____
_____
_____
_____
_____
_____
_____

I rate this book . . .

This drawing is a scene from the book. It shows . . .

_____

_____

_____

_____

_____

_____

BOOK TITLE:

Author

Illustrator

Fiction ☐ **Nonfiction** ☐ **# of Pages**

My favorite characters in the book are . . .

_____
_____
_____
_____

My favorite part of the book is . . .

_____
_____
_____
_____
_____
_____
_____

I rate this book . . .

☆ ☆ ☆ ☆ ☆ ☆ ☆ ☆ ☆ ☆

Date finished

This drawing is a scene from the book. It shows . . .

BOOK TITLE:

Author

Illustrator

Fiction ☐ Nonfiction ☐ # of Pages

My favorite characters in the book are . . .

_____

_____

_____

_____

My favorite part of the book is . . .

_____

_____

_____

_____

_____

_____

_____

I rate this book . . .

This drawing is a scene from the book. It shows . . .

_____

_____

_____

_____

_____

_____

BOOK TITLE:

Author

Illustrator

Fiction ☐　Nonfiction ☐　# of Pages

My favorite characters in the book are . . .

_____
_____
_____
_____

My favorite part of the book is . . .

_____
_____
_____
_____
_____
_____
_____

I rate this book . . .

☆ ☆ ☆ ☆ ☆ ☆ ☆ ☆ ☆ ☆

This drawing is a scene from the book. It shows . . .

BOOK TITLE:

Author

Illustrator

Fiction ☐   Nonfiction ☐   # of Pages

My favorite characters in the book are . . .

_____
_____
_____
_____

My favorite part of the book is . . .

_____
_____
_____
_____
_____
_____
_____
_____

I rate this book . . .

☆ ☆ ☆ ☆ ☆ ☆ ☆ ☆ ☆ ☆

This drawing is a scene from the book. It shows . . .

BOOK TITLE:

Author

Illustrator

Fiction ☐   Nonfiction ☐   # of Pages

My favorite characters in the book are . . .

_____
_____
_____
_____

My favorite part of the book is . . .

_____
_____
_____
_____
_____
_____
_____
_____

I rate this book . . . ☆ ☆ ☆ ☆ ☆ ☆ ☆ ☆ ☆

This drawing is a scene from the book. It shows . . .

_____

_____

_____

_____

_____

_____

BOOK TITLE:

Author

Illustrator

Fiction ☐ Nonfiction ☐ # of Pages

My favorite characters in the book are . . .

_____
_____
_____
_____

My favorite part of the book is . . .

_____
_____
_____
_____
_____
_____

I rate this book . . .

☆ ☆ ☆ ☆ ☆ ☆ ☆ ☆ ☆ ☆

This drawing is a scene from the book. It shows . . .

_____

_____

_____

_____

_____

_____

_____

BOOK TITLE:

Author

Illustrator

Fiction ☐   Nonfiction ☐   # of Pages

My favorite characters in the book are . . .

_____
_____
_____
_____

My favorite part of the book is . . .

_____
_____
_____
_____
_____
_____
_____
_____

I rate this book . . .

☆ ☆ ☆ ☆ ☆ ☆ ☆ ☆ ☆ ☆

This drawing is a scene from the book. It shows . . .

_____

_____

_____

_____

_____

_____

_____

BOOK TITLE:

Author

Illustrator

Fiction ☐   Nonfiction ☐   # of Pages

My favorite characters in the book are . . .

_____
_____
_____
_____

My favorite part of the book is . . .

_____
_____
_____
_____
_____
_____
_____
_____

I rate this book . . .

☆ ☆ ☆ ☆ ☆ ☆ ☆ ☆ ☆ ☆

This drawing is a scene from the book. It shows . . .

BOOK TITLE:

Author

Illustrator

Fiction ☐ **Nonfiction** ☐ **# of Pages**

My favorite characters in the book are . . .

_____
_____
_____
_____

My favorite part of the book is . . .

_____
_____
_____
_____
_____
_____
_____

I rate this book . . .

Date finished

This drawing is a scene from the book. It shows . . .

BOOK TITLE:

Author

Illustrator

Fiction ☐   Nonfiction ☐   # of Pages

My favorite characters in the book are . . .

_____
_____
_____
_____

My favorite part of the book is . . .

_____
_____
_____
_____
_____
_____
_____
_____

I rate this book . . .

☆ ☆ ☆ ☆ ☆ ☆ ☆ ☆ ☆ ☆

This drawing is a scene from the book. It shows . . .

_____
_____
_____
_____
_____
_____
_____

BOOK TITLE:

Author

Illustrator

Fiction ☐ **Nonfiction** ☐ **# of Pages**

My favorite characters in the book are . . .

_____
_____
_____
_____

My favorite part of the book is . . .

_____
_____
_____
_____
_____
_____
_____

I rate this book . . .

☆ ☆ ☆ ☆ ☆ ☆ ☆ ☆ ☆

This drawing is a scene from the book. It shows . . .

_____

_____

_____

_____

_____

_____

BOOK TITLE:

Author

Illustrator

Fiction ☐ Nonfiction ☐ # of Pages

My favorite characters in the book are . . .

_____
_____
_____
_____

My favorite part of the book is . . .

_____
_____
_____
_____
_____
_____
_____

I rate this book . . .

☆ ☆ ☆ ☆ ☆ ☆ ☆ ☆ ☆ ☆

This drawing is a scene from the book. It shows . . .

_____

_____

_____

_____

_____

_____

BOOK TITLE:

Author

Illustrator

Fiction ☐ Nonfiction ☐ # of Pages

My favorite characters in the book are . . .

_____
_____
_____
_____

My favorite part of the book is . . .

_____
_____
_____
_____
_____
_____
_____

I rate this book . . .

This drawing is a scene from the book. It shows . . .

_____

_____

_____

_____

_____

_____

_____

BOOK TITLE:

Author

Illustrator

Fiction ☐ Nonfiction ☐ # of Pages

My favorite characters in the book are . . .

_____
_____
_____
_____

My favorite part of the book is . . .

_____
_____
_____
_____
_____
_____
_____

I rate this book . . .

☆ ☆ ☆ ☆ ☆ ☆ ☆ ☆ ☆ ☆

This drawing is a scene from the book. It shows . . .

BOOK TITLE:

Author

Illustrator

Fiction ☐ **Nonfiction** ☐ **# of Pages**

My favorite characters in the book are . . .

_____
_____
_____
_____
_____

My favorite part of the book is . . .

_____
_____
_____
_____
_____
_____
_____
_____

I rate this book . . .

☆ ☆ ☆ ☆ ☆ ☆ ☆ ☆ ☆ ☆

This drawing is a scene from the book. It shows . . .

_____

_____

_____

_____

_____

_____

BOOK TITLE:

Author

Illustrator

Fiction ☐ Nonfiction ☐ # of Pages

My favorite characters in the book are . . .

_____
_____
_____
_____

My favorite part of the book is . . .

_____
_____
_____
_____
_____
_____
_____
_____

I rate this book . . .

☆ ☆ ☆ ☆ ☆ ☆ ☆ ☆ ☆ ☆

This drawing is a scene from the book. It shows . . .

BOOK TITLE:

Author

Illustrator

Fiction ☐ **Nonfiction** ☐ **# of Pages**

My favorite characters in the book are . . .

_____
_____
_____
_____

My favorite part of the book is . . .

_____
_____
_____
_____
_____
_____
_____

I rate this book . . .
☆ ☆ ☆ ☆ ☆ ☆ ☆ ☆ ☆ ☆

Date finished

This drawing is a scene from the book. It shows . . .

BOOK TITLE:

Author

Illustrator

Fiction ☐ **Nonfiction** ☐ **# of Pages**

My favorite characters in the book are . . .

_____
_____
_____
_____

My favorite part of the book is . . .

_____
_____
_____
_____
_____
_____
_____

I rate this book . . .

☆ ☆ ☆ ☆ ☆ ☆ ☆ ☆ ☆ ☆

This drawing is a scene from the book. It shows . . .

_____

_____

_____

_____

_____

_____

_____

BOOK 👉
TITLE:

Author

Illustrator

Fiction ☐ **Nonfiction** ☐ **# of Pages**

My favorite characters in the book are . . .

_____
_____
_____
_____

My favorite part of the book is . . .

_____
_____
_____
_____
_____
_____
_____

I rate this book . . .

☆ ☆ ☆ ☆ ☆ ☆ ☆ ☆ ☆ ☆

This drawing is a scene from the book. It shows . . .

BOOK 👉 TITLE:

Author

Illustrator

Fiction ☐ **Nonfiction** ☐ **# of Pages**

My favorite characters in the book are . . .

_____

_____

_____

_____

My favorite part of the book is . . .

_____

_____

_____

_____

_____

_____

_____

I rate this book . . .

☆ ☆ ☆ ☆ ☆ ☆ ☆ ☆ ☆ ☆

This drawing is a scene from the book. It shows . . .

_____
_____
_____
_____
_____
_____

BOOK TITLE:

Author

Illustrator

Fiction ☐ **Nonfiction** ☐ **# of Pages**

My favorite characters in the book are . . .

_____
_____
_____
_____

My favorite part of the book is . . .

_____
_____
_____
_____
_____
_____
_____

I rate this book . . .

☆ ☆ ☆ ☆ ☆ ☆ ☆ ☆ ☆ ☆

This drawing is a scene from the book. It shows . . .

Notes